Henry Lee Thomas

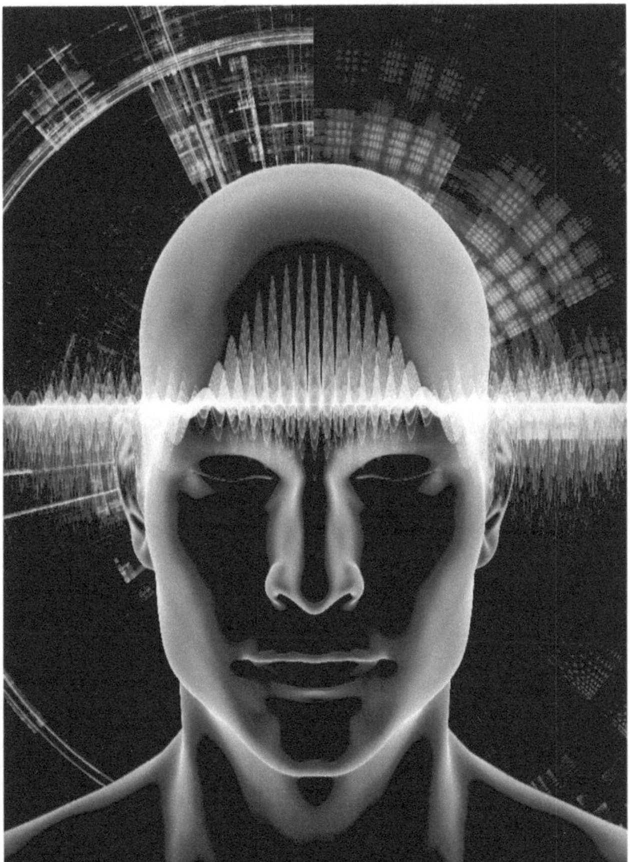

Mental Streams
Poems of the Heart and Soul

Mental Streams

Copyright © 2020 by Henry Lee Thomas.

All rights reserved. No part of this book may be reproduced in any form or by electronic means without permission in writing from the author.

Cover Design: Nabin Karna
Photos/Illustrations: Stock Photo Secrets
Editing: Evy Zen

Printed & bound in the United States of America

Library of Congress Control Number: 2020913101

Publisher's Cataloging-in-Publication Data
provided by Five Rainbows Cataloging Services

Names: Thomas, Henry Lee, author.
Title: Mental Streams: Poems of the Heart and Soul / Henry Lee Thomas.
Description: Manassas, VA: Henry Thomas, 2020.
Identifiers: LCCN 2020913101 (print) | ISBN 978-1-970144-03-1 (paperback) | ISBN 978-1-970144-04-8 (hardcover) | ISBN 978-1-970144-05-5 (ebook)
Subjects: LCSH: Flash fiction. | Poetry. | Short stories. | African Americans. | Men. | BISAC: POETRY / American / African American. | FICTION / Short Stories (single author) | POETRY / Subjects & Themes / Family.
Classification: LCC PS3620.H66 M46 2020 (print) | LCC PS3620.H66 (ebook) | DDC 813/.6--dc23.

www.MentalStreams.com
hthomas@notjustformen.com

Dedication

To all the people who are struggling in the darkness, look inside yourself to find the light.

To all the people who have lost love, if you open your heart you will find it again.

To all the people doing the heavy lifting in promoting peace, harmony, equality, and true justice. Thank you.

Legal Statement

This book is a work of fiction. Names, characters, and incidents either are products of the author's imagination or are used fictitiously. Any resemblance to actual events or persons, living or dead, is entirely coincidental.

**It is impossible to see very far ahead
of what life has in store for you.
That part of the path is always dark.**

- Henry Lee Thomas

Contents

INTRODUCTION 1
I: THE FIRST STREAMS 5
   Mental Stew 7
   Our World is A-Changing 8
   Mental Floss 10
   Don't Disrespect My Afro 11
   Poetry is Life 12
   Self-Worth 13
   The Landing 14
   Up & Down the Merry-Go-Round 16
   Black Dirt 17
   The Dollar Store 18
   Cell Phone Justice 19
   My First Day 20
   Stop the Madness 21
   Give Me Back My Dreams 22
   Police Officers Stand Up 24
   Path of Evil 25
   The Underground Railroad 26
   Route Your Way to Happiness 28
   Is This 1920 or 2020? 29
   Chewing On Toothpicks 30
   How Wars Are Won 31

You Had Me at "Please" 32
The Lost Art of the Compromise 33
Has Civil Rights Disappeared? 34
GOD 35
Why Are We Here? 36

II: FAMILY 39
One Seed 41
The Blood That Binds 42
Let's Celebrate the Rainbow 43
My Work Wife 44
Mates for Life 45
Ode to Mom 46
Ode to Dad 47
Dear Biracial Son 48
Evil Twin 50
Family Intelligence 51
Ode to the Great Indian Chiefs 52
Family Secrets 53
Black Blood Lines 54
Is There Life On Other Planets? 55
Ode to Robert Smalls 56
Family Affair 58
We Are One People 59

III: LOVE 61
My Lighthouse 63
Imagine My Surprise 64

Thoughts of You 65
Have Tea with Me 66
Whiskey and Tea 67
Love Syndrome 68
Please Hear Me 69
Close to You 70
Love is a Rose 71
Oh Baby let me Feel You Up 72
Don't Come Here 73
Love Train 74
The One in the Corner 75
With This Heart, I Do Wed 76
Musical Orgasm 77
Tell It to Me Straight 78
Separation 79
Lust to Love 80
Quarantine with Me 81
Love, Space, & Time 82
Blessed and Secure 83
On My Lonely Nights 84
Pure Love 85
Let Me Break It Down To You 86
Opposite 87
Haight-Ashbury 88
In the Mist of the Darkness 90
Busting Loose 91

White on Black	92
Black on Black	93
My Love Runneth Over	94
It's Not Like That	95
Love Jam	96
One Lonely Flower	97
Unlock Your Heart	98

IV: NATURE 99

Butterflies	101
Bluebirds	102
Deep in the Mountains	103
Red Wine	104
How the Wild Birds Sing	105
Water Lilies	106
Where the Wind Blows	107
The Core	108
The Beach	109
Fish at Play	110
The Air We Breathe	111
Soaking In the Sunshine	112
Desert Storms	113
Spring	114

V: THE FINAL STREAMS 115

The Mind	117
Life's Setbacks	118
Soap Opera	119

Don't Back the Wrong Leader	120
Ode to Bob Dylan	121
Soliloquy in Black	122
It's worse than I Thought	123
In Harm's Way	124
Mind Streams	125
Thank You	126
Easy Guideline for Giving	127
COVID-19	128
Senior Lives Matter	129
The 4th of July Is Not My Holiday	131
Small People	132
Peace	133
Dig Deep	134
That's Not Me	135
The Dark Side	136
Behind the Looking Glass	137
The Harlem Hellfighters	138
The Fate of My Dreams	139
Pick Me up Lord	140
Why Do You Disparage My Race?	141
Rise Up	142
Downstream	144
The Final Frontier	145
VI: FLASH FICTION STORIES	**147**
The House	149

Gone At 73 153
The Lucky Charm of My Success 155
Who is My Father? 157
ABOUT THE AUTHOR 159
What Did You Think of Mental Streams? 161

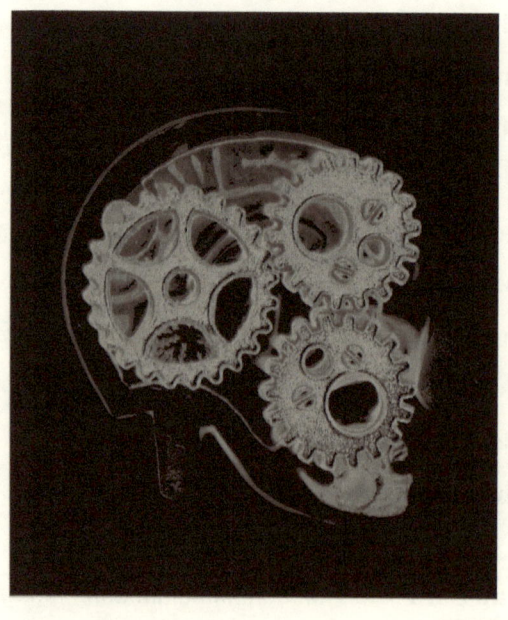

INTRODUCTION

The poetry in this book is a diverse mix of styles, thoughts, observations, and emotions which have emanated from my mind, all reflecting the realities of life.

We all experience love, hate, despair, joy, and loss. These are all emotions I have first-hand knowledge about and what I wanted to convey with this book.

Thus, with this effort I hope to take the reader on a journey which has meaning for them in multiple ways.

This collection is not just doom and gloom like a lot of poetry books though. There is some doom and gloom but there are also passages that give hope, good news, and shows that there is a light at the end of the tunnel.

To turn the dark into light though you need to roll up your sleeves and work to make things better – put in some elbow grease.

You can't stand on the sidelines. You need to get your hands dirty to be part of the solution. It's a journey of understanding, accepting and then getting down and doing something and calling out those who are on the wrong side of history.

The pieces are roughly grouped into sections which share a common theme though you will find exceptions as you read from beginning to end. If I was not sure which section to put a piece in, I dropped it in the first or last section whichever one seemed like a closer fit.

The first section is called "First Streams". It deals with "newness". New life, new way of thinking, new existence, or just the beginning of a new or needed change. It also documents some of my first thoughts as images and insights streamed through my consciousness.

The Family section deals with, *wait for it*, families. Families in all forms and permutations and the interactions, issues, and love they share.

The *Love* section? Well you know what that is. But do you see it in the same way I do? Love is love until it isn't. It also has many flavors and is a major focus in our lives.

The Nature section was a must as I am in love with nature and how it enhances and impacts the life we live. To truly maximize the beauty of life I believe you have to experience nature in all its wondrous forms.

The Final Streams section represents my final thoughts on an array of different topics in no particular order. I know, I could have come up with a more exciting name for this section (as well as the first section) but the poetry should be the focus, right?

I finish off this collection with a series of flash fiction stories as a bonus, a little bit of something extra for you to sink your teeth into. These flash stories provided me with a workshop to communicate a more robust feeling and emotion than is possible with the poetry selections. I end this book on that note.

I hope you enjoy this current collection and that at least some of them affect you in an emotional and meaningful way.

If you can be moved by poetry it can bring joy to your day, give you a deeper understanding of yourself and the world, as well as help you to navigate this thing we call life.

Thanks for purchasing my book. If after reading it you enjoyed it, please consider leaving an honest review at your favorite store or the site you purchased the book from.

Happy Reading and Peace Out!

Those who refuse
to see the light
will be forever
in the dark.

- Henry Lee Thomas

I: THE FIRST STREAMS

Mental Stew

Find the recipe.
Mix all the ingredients.
Bake your mental stew.

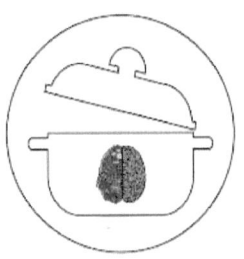

Our World is A-Changing

Listen up people.
It's time to be strong.
Let's go to the highest steeple
to shout out our new theme song.

Our world is a-changing.
It's no longer acceptable
to advocate bias and hate.
This is a new day
and we can no longer wait.

All people are created equal
and this we cannot deny.
So let's not create a sequel
to our past racist battle cry.

Our world is a-changing.
It's no longer acceptable
to advocate bias and hate.
This is a new day
and we can no longer wait.

Heed the current movement
to throw out all our racist symbols
and get on board with this revolution,
to send the right signals.

Our world is a-changing.
It's no longer acceptable
to advocate bias and hate.
This is a new day
and we can no longer wait.

Folks from all over the world,
representing all our human colors
and all the different nations,
have banded together as sisters and brothers.

The people have spoken
and they have voiced their desire,
to move the world forward
from our past quagmire.

Our world is a-changing.
It's no longer acceptable
to advocate bias and hate.
This is a new day
and we **won't** wait!

Mental Floss

Cut your mental floss.
Work it between your two ears.
Slide from side to side.

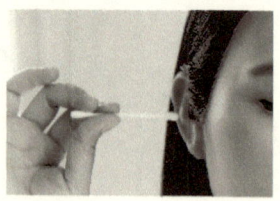

Don't Disrespect My Afro

Please don't disrespect my afro.
Why does it bother you so?
My hair doesn't need to be straight
in order for me to rate.

Maybe it makes you feel inferior
when you want to feel superior,
but your limp locks
just don't rock.

Get out your curling iron,
roll up your strands,
and then your hair will
look just like mine.

At the end of the day
all hair is okay
and it serves no purpose
to pretend it's any other way.

Poetry is Life

Poetry is life.

It originates from deep inside,
though it doesn't require two objects to collide.

To breathe life into it give it nourishment to survive
by injecting it with the emotion to thrive.

Its beauty may be present in the creator's eye
and sometimes it will make them cry.

But in order to garner a larger audience,
it cannot rely on the masses' clairvoyance.

It must touch the reader in a nurturing way
to make them want to stay.

Self-Worth

Everybody has worth.
Don't allow your self-worth to fade.
Don't limit the contributions you can make.
You are in control of your fate.

Your worth is not defined by your number of followers,
your number of Facebook friends,
or your number of likes.

We tend to place too much emphasis on the outside voices
instead of paying attention to our inner voice,
the one that knows your worth.

It's a state of mind
and you need to change yours
to find your mastermind.
If you do, you will find it worthwhile.

The Landing

They landed in 1619 at what was then known as Point Comfort in the Chesapeake area of Virginia.

Around 20 African Slaves were shipped there against their will from Angola and their arrival was their first survival.

They were traded by their captors for food and supplies while their freedom was being denied.

This is the place that later became the United States, where "all men are created equal." However, to justify their actions, these United States had to call these people chattel.

They arrived in a new land and were forced to work in a foreign one, while missing their homeland.

Their women were sometimes raped by their owners and the offspring which resulted were not recognized by their fathers.

Two of these slaves were Anthony and Isabela, who managed to survive and had a child called William.

The work must have been difficult, especially when you couldn't leave the gate and were subjected to hate.

It forces you to learn to survive in trying times, and to make your escape when you think it is safe.

They are honored today at Point Comfort, which is what Fort Monroe used to be called.

They are honored for their perseverance, ability to adapt, and courage to survive.

I wonder what the United States would look like today if they didn't have slaves who had to work without pay.

They may not have been able to keep the British at bay or have enough food, clothing, or weapons to fight another day.

Chances are it would be an academic question because without slaves and the contributions they made, there would be no USA.

Up & Down the Merry-Go-Round

You go up and down the merry go round
as its wary axis grinds against the ground.

You peter around without a frown
as your belly laughter mutes the sound.

When you think it may get off the ground,
you soon realize it has to be earthbound.

For if it could really reach for the sky,
surely all the fun would say goodbye.

Merry-go-rounds are not meant to fly
or helicopter away like a butterfly.

Their only purpose is to satisfy
the pleasure center of a child's desire.

Black Dirt

Black dirt is all they could see
when the old racists looked at me.
It wasn't in their nomenclature
to articulate on paper
a less demeaning designation.

Do they really believe
they are better than me?
Or is it that they don't want me to be free?

What they don't realize
is that black dirt is the best kind.
It provides nutrients and life to the soil.
It is the foundation of life
and the color of the original man.

It's time they realized the significance
of the black and tan
to the beauty of this land.

The Dollar Store

Bargains are to be found at the Dollar Store.
Everything used to be a dollar or less, but not anymore.
It's still a bargain, you just have to pay a little more.

It's the place for the financially challenged,
the minimum wage worker,
the people just starting out,
and oftentimes, people of color.

It's a world some of us do not know
because we are more secure and have more dough.
If you go there it's not a place you want to stay.
You hope to move on.

Graduating from the Dollar Store is a great day.
It means you have made it,
or at least you have some breathing room.
Yay, hurray!

We all have to survive any way we can.
One person isn't any better than the other
and you may find yourself there one day.

Do not judge, do not speculate.
If you see someone leaving the Dollar Store
say "Hi, have a great day."
If you are going in, keep your chin up.

Cell Phone Justice

In earlier days when crimes were committed
by a government official against a black citizen,
it was their word against the victim's.
The government official won.

In earlier days when crimes were committed
by white citizens against black citizens
it was the white citizen's word against the victim's.
The white citizen won.

Then along came cell phones with cameras.

Now when crimes are committed
by government officials or white citizens
against black citizens,
it's their word against the cell phone video.
The black citizen *should* win.

My First Day

It was my first day of school
and I was not in the mood.
I had to brush my teeth, wash my face, and tie my shoes.

It was a sunny day
but I couldn't go outside to play.
Dad went with me to drop me off
because he was the only one
who could keep me from running away.

As I entered the room where I was to be held prisoner
my dad waved goodbye and said, "Good luck mister!"
I scanned the room to see who else was there
and I noticed a girl with the most beautiful hair.

I looked at her with a steady glare
as she tossed her hair back with an extra flair.

She returned my look with her freckled smile
and said hello with lots of style.

At this point I leaned back in my chair,
finally happy to begin my new school affair.

Stop the Madness

There has been an increase
in bigotry and hate,
including divisive signs
and racially motivated crimes.

That's not who we are as a nation:
To condone hate
or to support its symbols.

If Lady ~~Antebellum~~
and The ~~Dixie~~ Chicks *get it*,
why can't you?

I know it can be hard
to muster the strength
to do the right thing,
but we must.

We need to do a gut check
to find it in ourselves
to break the bottleneck.

Let's open up our hearts
to let the love flow
and stop the madness.

Give Me Back My Dreams

Give me back my dreams.

The ones I used to make in bed
while I was waiting to go to sleep
but the suspense was keeping me awake.

How could I have known that
forces had been put in place
to blockade my effort to succeed?

How do I overcome the obstacles
when victory is stacked against me
with bricks as high as the Eiffel Tower?

It shouldn't be this way.

It should be an even playing field,
not a stacked deck.

It's hard to focus
when the thick air of bias
is breathing down my neck.

There has to be a set of countermeasures
which allows me to circumnavigate the blockage,
but the path seems to go on and on.

I can't give up on what I still desire
and what I have a right to possess.

Don't hold me back from the attacks
which are puncturing me,
just let me bleed.

The rat-a-tat-tat on my back
will help focus my will
to fight back and stay on track.

I won't give up,
but I could use some help
from those who realize
the role they are playing
puts them on the wrong side.

Dreams are made to enhance our lives,
to help us to strive to be better,
and to realize our potential.
I will not be broken.

Police Officers Stand Up

Police officers we need you to stand up
for what you know is right.

I believe that most of you are true blue
but you can't continue to shelter your comrades
who are over-ripe.

You can't keep on supporting the bad apples in your force
because one rotten apple spoils the whole corps.

If you stand by us we will stand by you.

The good officers should not be blamed for what the bad ones do, but it is difficult not to do when there is no accountability for the bad few.

We are in this together and we should all want the same thing: Liberty and justice for all.

Let's stand together in a united front to expose the bad apples on both sides and to stand committed to make things better.

Path of Evil

The path of evil is always around
trying to destroy the moral ground.
It is there in front of you,
ready to pounce.

It comes in the form of
racism, bigotry, intolerance,
and the will to do harm.

We always have a choice
of which route to take:
The evil dirt road or the moral interstate.

If enough of us take the high road
the evil road will dissipate.
We must keep evil routes at bay
so they won't survive another day.

The Underground Railroad

The Underground Railroad
was not a road at all,
it was the path to freedom
for the enslaved crowd.

There were many different routes
which originated in the South
and headed north
to the "free" states and Canada.

A few even fled to Mexico and Florida
before Florida became part of
the United States.

It was a dangerous journey
and if caught they could be killed,
but if they stayed their life would be nil.

These "Passengers" stopped
at many "Stations",
which were places of safety
on their way to salvation.

These Stations were
people's homes or businesses
and even included
Oberlin College,
which was a place of knowledge.

The train "Conductors" were
red, white, and black;
free and enslaved;
who believed in human rights.

The most famous Conductor
was Harriet Tubman
who helped free over 70 people
from slavery's crutches.

The railroad saved many lives
but those who escaped
were replaced by new arrivals.

This slavery thing was
a huge black mark
on the United States
quest for equality.

For if you don't believe in
freedom for all,
all you are doing
is setting yourself
up for a fall.

Route Your Way to Happiness

If you are seeking happiness
you need to pull out a map
and plan out your route
to make sure you get there.

You can't rely on others,
as they can't know where you want to go
or how you want to get there.
It's up to you to find your own way
so you can get there without delay.

So roll up your sleeves
and determine your needs,
so you can get there with Godspeed.

Is This 1920 or 2020?

Is this 1920 or 2020?

1920: America's isolationist philosophy after WWI.
2020: Isolationism creeps back into the United States.

1920: Resurgence of the KKK.
2020: Resurgence of the KKK.

1920: The National Origins Act severely restricts foreigners entering the United States.
2020: Proclamation to suspend immigration into the United States.

1920: J. Edgar Hoover of the FBI started his unsubstantiated conspiracy theories.
2020: An unsubstantiated conspiracy theory that 75 old protester, Martin Gugino, was an ANTIFA provocateur.

1920: Effort to fight passage of the 19th Amendment, giving Women the right to vote.
2020: Forces trying to suppress the minority vote.

1920: Denial and uncertainty about the 1918-20 Spanish Flu pandemic by political leaders.
2020: Denial and uncertainty about the 2020-? COVID-19 pandemic by political leaders.

You be the judge…

Chewing On Toothpicks

Chewing on toothpicks is what I need
in order for my mind to breathe.
It warms my head and puts me at ease,
and protects me against brain freeze.

As I chew away and take my time
my thoughts begin to fall in line,
enabling me to reach a different state,
which allows me to meditate.

I am then able to negotiate
with my inner self
to find peace of mind.

How Wars Are Won

Wars are not won by military might.
They are won by changes in a person's mindsight.
That is, a person's ability to have insight
into themselves and empathy for others' plight.

Winning the battle is only the beginning.
If attitudes are not changed,
the battlefield is just rearranged.

The Union Army won the Civil War
but they didn't win the war for equality.
Thus, the war for equal treatment goes on.

For over 155 years after the end of the Civil War
the search for equality is still a chore.
We failed to follow up with the needed curriculum
to change the mind and souls,
and to make our nation whole.

We need to bring this fight to the schools
by teaching our children that when we say
"all men are created equal", we really mean **All Men**.
Regardless of color, sex or other persuasions,
we should be "all for one and one for all".

If we can execute the above
and protect our minorities from the ones who hate,
we will finally win the most important war.

You Had Me at "Please"

Some people rarely say please
because they don't see the need
to get what they want.

They don't realize
they can get so much more
if their request starts with *please*.

It's a reflection of the world we are in
that this tendency exists,
but we must find a fix.

For I am more likely to assist you
when your request starts with *please*.

That is why when you asked me to please help
and went through the motion
to convince me to comply,
I told you:
"You had me at please".

The Lost Art of the Compromise

We seem to have misplaced
the art of the compromise.

For all we see
in the current time
is the art of the divide.

Like pushing in opposite directions
and being surprised there is no progress,
it should occur to us that
we should push in the same direction
or agree on an alternate route.

It's not too late,
but we all must
join in the search
to find that lost art
to save the day.

Has Civil Rights Disappeared?

There appears to be an increase in the amount of violence against Black people in 2019 and 2020.

How can this be over 50 years after the Civil Rights Acts of 1964 and 1968?

How can this be after the election of a Black president of the good ole USA?

Has civil rights disappeared or has the desire to enforce them been smeared?

We used to sing "we shall overcome". Maybe we need a new fight song.

The good news is that the world is beginning to see what Black people already knew. That injustices are committed against people of color, from bias and unequal treatment to knees on the collar.

Hurray for cameras for bringing this to light, but let's not squander the opportunity to end this fight.

GOD

Give your best effort.

Open up your heart.

Do the right thing.

Why Are We Here?

Have you ever wondered why we are here?
What is the purpose of the human race on this earth?
Other lifeforms with brains appear to have a purpose,
at a minimum, to be part of a food chain.

Snakes eat rats, owls eat snakes (and rats).
Crabs eat plankton, sharks eat crabs (and humans).
Giraffes eat leaves, lions eat giraffes.
You get the picture…

In general, lower-level lifeforms perform some function
to make life possible for higher lifeforms
and to provide diversity to the planet.

But if you are at the top of the food chain,
what is your purpose?
We humans do provide some diversity
and that is a good thing,
but why do we have the big brain we have?
Is it to rule over the other animals
because they need a king or queen?

Maybe our purpose is to make the world better,
to leave it in a better place than when we were born.
If so this would need to be a group effort
to be successful, as we could not do it alone.

But we can do what we can.
This role requires us to be good citizens.
That means no fighting, no racism,
and no putting people down.

We need to build each other up,
fight for our common good,
help each other out, and be tolerant.

At the end of the day we need to be able to say
"I have made a positive contribution on this earth
and I left it in better shape than when I was born".

If we can't do this our life would have been a failure
and you don't get another shot at success.
There are no life do-overs.

**There is always
a way forward
as long as you
stay the course.**

- Henry Lee Thomas

II: FAMILY

One Seed

We all originated from one seed.

If you know that, act like it.

If you don't know it, believe it.

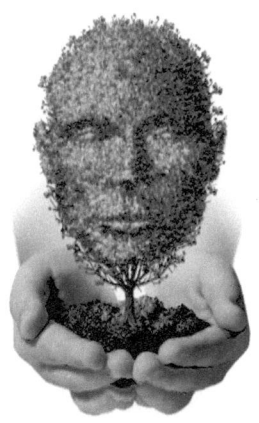

The Blood That Binds

Rarely do I ponder the meaning of family
or think about the humble beginnings
their members have in genesis.

Some are close and some or not.
So it's not always clear why we should plant a seed
to band together as a united breed.
Which leads some to believe it's all a plot
to fool one into believing there *is* a need.

But I think that's all bull,
as I feel a strong uncontrollable pull
to surrender my unfaltering faith
and focus my beliefs and mind
on the blood that binds.

Let's Celebrate the Rainbow

Let's celebrate the rainbow
of human colors and sexes we have.

From white to black
and from male to female,
there are no drawbacks
to this diversity attack.

White is nice,
yellow is mellow,
red is sacred,
brown is renown,
black is profound,
the sexes are unique,
and all the above belong
to keep us strong.

There is a reason for
nature's zeal in creating
the human color and sex wheels:
It protects us against the unknown
to diversity the human genome.

My Work Wife

I remember the first day I met my work wife…
It was in the company breakroom as I was looking for ice.
She sashayed right in and caught my eye.
As our eyes met, we both said hi.

We began working together all day long
and we were very good at getting along.
We were birds of a feather
and often ate lunch together.
We spent more time with each other,
than we did with our mates.
The only difference was we didn't go on dates.

As time went on it was difficult to see
the difference between these two beings.
My home wife was great, yes indeed,
but my work wife was supplying more of my needs.

It was time to shift my distribution of needs
back to where they really belong.
Because that is where they really should be
and it will keep my marriage from being short-lived.

Mates for Life

An estimated 5% of all mammals mate for life, which doesn't give me a warm and fuzzy feeling that you will always be my wife.

Beavers, wolves, bats, and foxes are part of the select 5% but we all know what humans do.

Some of us only mate with one person at a time, while others can end up anywhere at bedtime.

Many of us stay together for the children, but some still get a little bit on the side.

It's such a difficult thing to do, to stay together as just one crew.

But some of us need to take one for the team, so we can raise our children and extend the human dream.

For the sake of our kids, and the love we feel, let's make our family part of the select few.

Ode to Mom

When life finds you down and out of your mind,
and you don't see a way of rebounding,
your mom is the one you will need to find.
She is the one to give you the grounding.

Even though you feel like you are drowning,
her memory will bring you peace of mind.
Open your eyes and check your surroundings
to search for all the blessings you can find.

This will stop your head from pounding
as you see she has not left you behind.
For even if she is not around,
her motherly presence will always be divine.

Ode to Dad

Dad has given me the strength to survive.
He is a man I would be proud to be.
He exuded dignity but didn't take jive.
He taught me why all men should be free.

To have the freedom to prosper and thrive
he worked six day weeks with unflinching glee
to feed his tribe and to keep us alive,
but bias forces would not let him be.

However, they were not able to dampen his drive.
Some would like to hang him from a tree,
but he always protected us in his hive.
Thank goodness for his ability to remain free.

Dear Biracial Son

Dear Biracial Son,

It is unfortunate that you decided to listen to others
and not heed my messages and creed.

As a black man who has experienced a lot, my knowledge
would have fed your needs.

Instead, you allowed your mother to lead you astray.

Why did you believe your white mother over me?

Surely you could not have fallen for the faulty belief
that blacks will only deceive.

Don't you realize that you are black like me?

I tried to teach you all you needed to survive
but you decided that you were smarter than me.

I told you about the racism and obstacles I had to endure and
what you needed to do to make your future secure.

You had all the tools you needed to excel
but like many conflicted children you decided to rebel.
It would have been better if you had used your brain
to put your faith in dad.

You didn't see the benefit of being a renaissance man and
decided to be a madman instead.

You don't understand the issues you will have
without an education at hand.
Not just an education from school,
but the education of the world in which you have to stand.

How do you plan to survive
when all your beliefs are based on lies?

Lies you chose to believe from others
because you thought they would make your life better.

In time you will begin to see the fallacy of your thoughts and
all the headaches they would have brought.

For the world will not be tolerant of your entitled air
and blaming me will just keep your cupboards bare.

It's time to take responsibility for your current state
and not procrastinate before it's too late.
It's also time to leave those negative forces behind
to improve your current state of mind.

Be careful how you act
lest you end up dead for being black.

I know the only way you will get the message
is if you have to fend for yourself.
Then you will see the wisdom of my message
verses everyone else's.

The decision is yours. I hope it's the right one.
Because which path you take will determine your fate.

Evil Twin

We all have an evil twin
who's trying to find an edge.
We harbor it with chagrin,
because it tries to draw a wedge.

It is not clear if we are born with it
or if it is the result of our environment,
but we can't let it make a base hit
or else it would be a worriment.

You must make sure your actions are pure
so you don't follow your evil self.
For if you are not sure,
you are at risk of losing yourself.

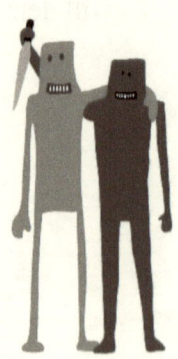

Family Intelligence

See me, see us.
We are a family and having your attention is a must.
Realize that this union must be based on total trust.

You need to manage your emotions
and not treat me as a token.
Please honor your family blessings
with emotional intelligence.

You are not regulating yourself in an empathetic way
and making me feel just okay.
What's motivating you to not show me respect?
Slow down buddy and don't be a clown
or else I won't stick around.

Ode to the Great Indian Chiefs

We celebrate the great Indian Chiefs
who roamed their native lands.
They held the highest beliefs
in their ability to command.

Sitting Bull, Geronimo, Cochise,
Joseph Brant, American Horse,
and many others.

They all fought with purpose
to preserve their way of living
by attempting to defeat outside forces,
who violated their oath of Thanksgiving.

We must not forget
their exceptional will to survive
or their right to fight
to protect their native lands.

The *First* Americans.

Family Secrets

Family secrets are meant to be kept
which can make you feel entrapped,
not being able to let it out
in fear of having a blowout.

The damage they can cause can be severe
and can cloud up the family atmosphere.
But the victims impacted have to suffer
so they can keep the secrets undercover.

Maybe it's time to open the door
to let in the light into this family gore.
For if you do it will set you free,
allowing your healing to soar.

Black Blood Lines

As I follow my black blood lines
back into time
I can see the struggles
we had to survive.

Working on plantations
and understanding our station,
while helping to save our nation,
so we could find salvation.

Fighting for our freedom
and trying not to be beaten,
we stood the test of time
because our movement was divine.

It's only a matter of time
that we will finally find acceptance
as an equal part of the human race.

Is There Life On Other Planets?

There are 100 billion planets in the Milky Way galaxy populating the skies in rhapsody.

There are 200 billion galaxies in the Universe randomly being interspersed.

There are around 10^{24} planets in our observable Universe. Said another way, there are:

    1,000,000,000,000,000,000,000,000 planets in the Universe.

To say that life only exists on earth is absurd.

It's not a question of is there life on other planets, but, where is life on other planets?

Ode to Robert Smalls

Robert Smalls was a South Carolina slave
and was born on Henry McKee's plantation.
He played in the McKee family enclave
because he was Henry McKee's son.

At age 15, he worked the Charleston city dock
and joined the crew of the ship CSS Planter,
where he also met his future wife Hannah.

He decided it was time for him to take stock
and to move his life to a different chapter
by fleeing the barbaric southern savannah.

He plotted to steal the ship at night
while the white crew were out on the town.
His family and slave crew started their flight
as they left the harbor with their heads down.

He evaded the enemy lines
by knowing the right signal
and imitating the real captain's stewardship.

He gave the Union ships the surrender sign
with the universal white flag symbol,
and provided the Union with a new ship.

Robert Smalls was a hero
at the dismay of the South.
He turned them into a zero
by punching them in the mouth.

He became a Navy Captain and congressman
and fought for civil rights after the war's end.

He returned to his homeland to continue his fight though he befriended his previous owners because he didn't come back with a gripe.

Family Affair

Vast is the universe
which binds the stars
in an infinite merge
while trying to converge.

It's a universal system
of competing tribes.
Kindred spirits
prancing the skies
while being careful
not to collide.

If only we could see
the force that emcees
this family tree.

The beautiful brood
descended from afar
which binds our existence
in their delicate sphere.

We are all connected
in this wondrous world
in which we find ourselves
in a family affair.

We Are One People

We are one people.
Red, yellow, white, brown, and black,
we all share a common track.

From deep in Africa to the seven seas,
we have changed our colors but not our breed.

From the inside, we can't tell each other apart
and our outside differences are a small sliver
of the human pie chart.

If we recognize our commonality
and celebrate our differences,
we will optimize the existence of our common lives.

**If you find yourself
in a dark place
turn on the light.**

- Henry Lee Thomas

III: LOVE

My Lighthouse

You are my lighthouse:
emitting your light of love,
saving me from life's dangers,
navigating me into your pleasures,
providing safe harbor for my thoughts,
and delivering me from a life of darkness.

Let's agree to shelter in place,
to join forces together,
to face all obstacles
as one.

Imagine My Surprise

Imagine my surprise
when I realized
my passion for you.

And then to understand,
from your message at hand,
that you feel it too.

It is rare that you find
two people so fine
with the same thing in mind
at the same moment in time.

Let's not delay
to put our love in play
on this very day.

Thoughts of You

Thoughts of you
come out of the blue
causing my heart to shake
because of what I might lose.

I know you are not sure
if I am right for you
but you should trust your gut
and follow its cue.

Our love is the cure
for the emptiness
we both have endured.

Please don't hesitant
to make the move
to allow me to prove
that our love is true.

Have Tea with Me

Have tea with me
under the banyan tree
so we can have a cup
and yuk-it-up.

After the clowning is done
we can turn around
and talk profoundly
about my feelings for you.

I want to plant a seed
within thee
so we can germinate
a new being.

If you feel the same
let's finish our tea
and make our tree.

Whiskey and Tea

Whiskey and tea
are good to me
as both have a stimulating effect.

They make me feel
confident and free,
and primed for what comes next.

The whiskey warms me up
and makes my rap silky smooth
as I prepare to have a cup of tea with you.

The tea allows me to
brew my thoughts
as I contemplate
my next move.

When both drinks are complete
and we are in the mood
we finish our time together
in the bedroom.

Love Syndrome

What is this syndrome that I possess?
It's called love but it is
making me a mess.

It feels like the flu
when I am not with you
but it feels divine
when you are by my side.

Am I supposed to be blue
and missing you
when I should be happy
since our love is new?

To have both good and bad
symptoms must be rare.
But why would anyone
subject themselves
to a love affair?

For you I am willing to bear the pain
for all the loving feelings I will gain.

Please Hear Me

Please hear me.
Don't think you know what I am thinking
without listening to me.

Please hear me.
Don't think you know what's best for me.

Please hear me.
I have a brain and I know what I want.

Please hear me.
Drop your assumptions and readings
of my body language.

Please hear me.
Treat me like an equal and respect me.

Please hear me.
If you don't hear me, I will leave you.

Do you hear me now?

Close to You

I want to be so close to you
that you feel me up
like an inner tube.

To be so close to you that
our hearts sync up
and carry the same beat.

To make love to you
in a tight embrace while
feeling your pulse with each thrust.

It's the closeness I cherish
and I hope this union
will last forever.

Love is a Rose

Love is a rose,
thorns and all.
It's a beautiful thing
unless one starts to stonewall.

Smells of rose, violet, jasmine, and other scents
parallel the different moods in the relationship.

If you make it thorn-free
you will have more glee.
But if it evolves into a cactus
it can be stickier.

You can turn it around
if it's meant to be
but you don't want to drown
if it's not meant to be.

It's a difficult thing to analyze,
to determine if it is divine.

The way to tell if it will sail
is to follow your heart and give it a sniff,
for if it's not right it will smell a little stale.

Oh Baby let me Feel You Up

Oh baby, let me feel you up
and satisfy my number one dream.

My mind is going crazy
and you're in my bloodstream.

I'm in a cold sweat
and feeling your steam.
Waiting is too much
and I just want to scream.

You know how much I want you
and it's a common theme.

I have told you many times before
and I know it's extreme.

But I will keep telling you
with a focused beam.

So drop your resistance and let me in
and allow me to complete my loving dream.

Don't Come Here

Don't come here looking for me
cause I don't want to hear your plea.

You had your chance
and you blew it.

What makes you think
you get a second dance?

Time is money and you
don't get any honey.

Please spare me from
your lying tales.

You showed your true colors
and I no longer want to be
your significant other.

So au revoir, adios!
I am through with you, lover.

Love Train

Hey baby, please get on my love train.
I'm coming into the station
to start my campaign
and to commence my flirtation.

All you need to do is get on board
to get a first-class seat
so we can strike a chord
in our private suite.

You won't regret
this smooth ride
as we work up a sweat
until we are tired.

So enjoy the view
as we choo choo away
and bid adieu
to the congested highway.

The One in the Corner

I want you, the one in the corner.
The one with the piercing eyes
and inviting smile.

The one who brings me joy and pride,
who makes me feel I am living in style.

The one I have cared for all my adult life,
whom I want to take down the wedding aisle.

Let's take our hands and move on out
to that center circle we have heard about.

With This Heart, I Do Wed

With this heart I do wed:
your body, mind, and soul.

A body that breaks the mold.
A mind to extol.
A soul to behold.

I accept all of you
with all of me
to be with thee.

Let's set the stage
to be engaged
in everlasting bliss.

Musical Orgasm

Music makes me quiver in the moonlight.
With its modulating cadence and subtle spice,
it gives credence to my pagan delights.

Its deceptive changes in key and pitch
forces my body into a mighty twitch.
As I anticipate the start of the first bridge,
I move in syncopation on your curving ridge.

The disturbance in the rhythm I feel
lets me know I am experiencing the real deal.
As it reaches the peak of its crescendo
I reach the end of my orgasmic concerto.

Tell It to Me Straight

Tell it to me straight
that you are not that into me.
I'm a big boy. I can take it.
No chaser required.
It's going to burn anyway.

No need to perpetuate
the falsity that you care.

Tell it like it is
so we can break the bond
that never was.

I am willing to let you go
so you can place your bets
on another dude.

I wish you well.
Take care,
adieu.

Separation

Separating from you is hard to do,

Especially since our love is new.

Please take this time to think

About the good times we had which were true.

Rest assured that I will not go away,

And we will be back together another day.

Time apart may bring us closer together,

Instead of pushing us farther away.

One thing that I hope and pray for is

Neither one of us will go astray.

Lust to Love

Lust is a spoken word
which implies that real feelings are being deferred.
But a lust feast may not be a bad meal
if it gives you some nourishment.
It's not very filling though,
as it doesn't have any fiber.
It's gone as soon as it is over.
No staying power.
No flow.

I want to feel something though,
but I also want substance.
Something to stick to my bones
and that makes me moan.
I will continue to look for more
until I can change that four letter word
from lust to love.

Quarantine with Me

There is a contagion out there causing fear
even though some people don't believe it's real.
It's been with us for almost a year
causing a lot of people to grieve.

You and I are currently alone
and trying to make the best of the situation.
We have been singing our sad song
while trying to deal with this aberration.

Your house and mine are fairly close
and you know how fond I am of you.
I think that you also hold me dear
so maybe we can help each other get through this.

Both of our temperatures are find, I see,
so come on baby and quarantine with me.

Love, Space, & Time

Love, space, and time:
The three steps we need to climb.

The love that reaches a higher state.
The space to give our love a break.
The time to allow our love to bake.

These three ingredients are all we need
to settle into a blissful ease.
But we must always remember to heed,
to respect each other with loving deeds.

Blessed and Secure

Blessed and secure
is how I feel
when I'm with you.

All hell can be breaking loose
and everyone else can be feeling blue,
but I will feel good with you.

I don't want this feeling to end
and I will do what I can
to make you want to stay too.

So I dedicate this day
in front of you
to my perpetual effort
to love you through and through.

On My Lonely Nights

On my lonely nights,
when no one else is in sight,
I search for insight into my plight.

What brings me here to this lonely site?
Does it feel right?

It would be nice to see another's face,
to share an intimate space,
to have someone else to embrace.

It does allow me to think out loud
without distractions or crowds.
It is sometimes beneficial to fill the void
with my unfiltered self
to not be destroyed.

I should make good use of this time
so that when the clock winds down
I am ready to be with you.

Pure Love

My love for you is
as pure as ivory soap
and makes me feel
as if I am floating on air.

When I think of you
I think of bubble baths
because sometimes you need one
to relax and not despair.

My love for you is as pure as
a freshly washed blanket
which I wrap around you
to keep you warm.

My love for you is
like pure gold
whose value just
continues to grow.

Know that
my thoughts are pure
when I tell you that
I love you
with all my heart.

Let Me Break It Down To You

Let me break it down to you
that I am loving the way you are doing it.
With your intelligent mind,
a face so divine,
and a figure which makes men
stop on a dime;
you are all that you can be.

Don't get me wrong
I know you are not here just for me
but if you want to give me some of your time
I am perfectly down with it.

You exude all that is good in a being
and all that I want for me.

I want to capture this moment
I have with you
and store it away
to always view.

If you allow me the opportunity
to see you again,
hopefully it will be as
more than friends.

Opposite

The opposite of pleasure is pain.
Sometimes you have to experience the latter,
to appreciate the former.

But other times pain *is* pleasure
as long as it doesn't go too far.
Pleasure is love.
Pain is hate?

Love your pleasure,
but don't hate your pain.

Haight-Ashbury

I remember when we were in our 20s:
In love with the world and each other.
We were flower children on a love trip
as we made our way to LA
in my brown MGB along Route 66.

I remember the smell of
chrysanthemums in your hair
and your flamboyant flair,
as we raced down the highway
without fanfare.

It was a glorious day
when we pulled into Santa Monica
as I treated my nostrils
to the ocean air.

We purchased 101 peace lilies
to distribute along the way
as we took Route 101 through the many cities.

It was the *"Summer of Love"*
and we needed to get to San Francisco
to join in the experience
of crafting new world goals.

As we rolled into Haight-Ashbury
it was an amazing scene,
as thousands of flower children
had convened.

We saw people from all over the world
and there was a fervor and passion in the air
that we could not have foreseen.

We loved, we laughed.
We drank, we smoked.
We listened to music, we talked.

We discussed the things that
were wrong with the world:
The hate, the bias, the selfishness,
and the value systems.

At the end of the stay
we had formulated a new world view.
We left with love and hope
and we returned with
new styles, behaviors, and ideas
to introduce to the world;
with high hopes of creating
a new world consciousness.

It didn't work. Maybe now it will…

In the Mist of the Darkness

In the mist of the darkness for all to see
is the blight light of your soul that I seek.

To fill the void with my soulmate
will turn the darkness into day.

Nothing else matters when our love is true
which helps to turn my dark skies blue.

Let's clear the mist so I can be with you
and we can turn up the fire on our love brew.

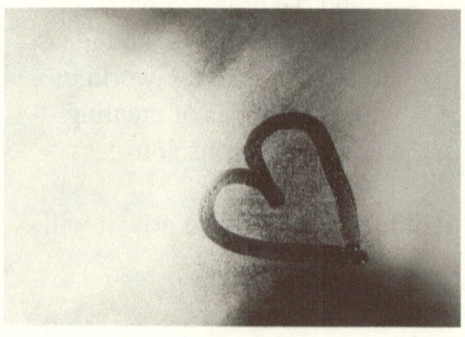

Busting Loose

I am busting loose with my love for you.
Letting it out feels about right.
I want to shout it out
so it can take flight
and turn my dark nights
into daylight.

It's the right thing.
It's the real deal.
It has great appeal.

I want to dance my life away
with you in my sights
feeding my soul
with your wondrous delights.

White on Black

Your white skin
on my black body
is my antibody.

You protect my immune system
with your love serum.

Your pure white skin like ivory soap
floats my boat and helps me cope.

Our two colors fit well together
like a checkerboard made in heaven.

Don't fight the contrast
and don't be harassed,
for our love is unsurpassed.

You are my light
in the darkest night
so let's love with all our might.

Black on Black

Lying next to you,
black on black,
almost gives me a heart attack.

The sparks fly high
when I touch your thigh
as we look up at the midnight sky.

I love the way we fit together,
not knowing where I end
or you begin.

I love being so close to you
that air cannot escape
and I can feel your bodyscape
as it drapes me from head to toe.

You are my Queen
and I am your King,
so let us continue to reign.

My Love Runneth Over

My love for you runneth over.

It is more than I could have hoped for
and more than I deserve.

Like the overflowing waters of Niagara Falls
and the reverberating sounds in a concert hall,
my love for you makes a big splash like rainfall.

Never could I have imagined
the span of my love for you
as it pierced my heart
and permeated my soul.

I want it to flow forever
as it percolates over,
down hills and dales,
into the recesses of
your love spell.

It's Not Like That

I know you think that
I don't want to commit,
but it's not like that.

We have been together a year
but we are still in first gear.
I only see you once a month
because you are rarely here.
I know you want to advance your career
but you are not treating me as a peer.

You say you want to increase our pace
but we hardly ever embrace.
I sense that you are afraid
that you could be played.

You have to lose the fear
so we can progress into a higher sphere.

It's time to open up your sails
so our relationship can thrive,
and we can move into love overdrive.

Love Jam

I want to dance with you
in a love jam for two.
Let's get the party started.

Don't stop the music
and let's keep on cruising.

Let's make a sweet mess
while working up a sweat
below the crescent moon.

As the rhythm ignites our groove
let's continue to dance the night away.

One Lonely Flower

I see one lonely flower
quivering in the breeze.
She's all by herself
like she was put away on a shelf.

I can feel her sorrow
being left alone,
like a single fish
in a big lagoon.

She reminds me of another
I used to know
who pushed me away
for reasons I never knew.

I think I can see a tear
dripping off her bloom.
I wonder how long
she can stand erect
in her lonely state
without a mate.

It must be someone
from a different crew.
But when I look closer,
I realize it's you.

Unlock Your Heart

My love, I know that you have been hurt before
and that you are reluctant to let me in.

I understand your fear
to depart to a new frontier
where the outcome is unclear
and your life could become austere.

But life is not worth living
if you don't open up to the possibility
of experiencing love.

I believe you have the strength
to survive if love goes amiss,
so give it a chance
in case it is a hit.

I can tell you that I am also
taking a risk
that my love for you
won't be requited.

But I am willing to take the risk
because I believe in us.

Please take a leap of faith
and unlock your heart
so our union can consummate.

IV: NATURE

Butterflies

Butterflies fly low
to reach the flowers below,
eat pollen and go.

Bluebirds

Bluebirds' twerking in the morning sky
bringing joy and love to everyone's life.

Searching for happiness with a glorious eye
while singing songs with a virtuous cry.

The harbinger of blessedness for thy
and also known as the spirit in the sky.

Blue-rose plumage which fills their chest
makes for a very handsome family crest.

Lest you think they are not the best,
you will find they are a desirable guest.

Keeping out foes and annoying pests
to make your home a happy nest.

Deep in the Mountains

Deep in the mountains
as they were covered with snow,
I found peace and flow.

Red Wine

Red wine is a favorite of mine.

It's a color of nature and oh so fine.

The rich deep hue can match one's lips

and the luscious taste is made for sipping.

It is the color of love, desire, and passion.

It has the taste of flowers, berries, and herbs.

It is the drink of kings and queens

as well as lovers and monks.

With all of this pleasure

it's hard to measure,

the value of this

fermented

juice.

How the Wild Birds Sing

Have you noticed how the wild birds sing?
They sing as if they don't have a care in the world
and without fear of rejection or self-consciousness.

This is the natural way.
The way it was meant to be.
No one teaches them to hold back
or parse their words.

We could learn something from them:
To not allow others to silence us,
to speak our mind,
to express ourselves in our own voice.

Take a page from the wild bird's playbook
and write your own song in your own words.
That's the way it was meant to be.

Water Lilies

There are water lilies in my pond
floating in an irresistible bond.
They creep together with their underwater stems
while proudly showing their fragrant flower gems.

How I wish I could float like them,
to experience the feeling of sweet succumb,
meditating in the water's abyss
while attracting my mate with a sun-drenched kiss.

To ripen the fruit of my lover's nest
until the seed of our love feeds on her breast.
To exalt in the beauty of our family flat
as we progress through life in our perennial habitat.

Where the Wind Blows

Somewhere in the sky
or deep in earth's lowest caverns
it takes a deep yawn,
opens its eyes,
and wonders:
Where will I blow today?

It is the wind.
It blows through fields,
it blows through valleys,
and it blows everywhere.

You can feel the breeze on your skin,
you can see it move the trees,
you can see it twist and weave,
and you can even feel it when you sneeze.

It's a force of nature
and should be taken seriously.
It can be gentle
or it can be strong.
If it's gentle play along,
but if it is strong,
it's time to be gone.

The Core

Our earth is hot under the collar
and has a fiery ball at its core.

If you were there you could hear it roar
as its heat began to soar.

It reminds me of that other place
where the devil hosts the disgraced.

Once you are there you can't come back
because you are permanently off track.

So make the best of life while you can
because you could end up in Satan's hands.

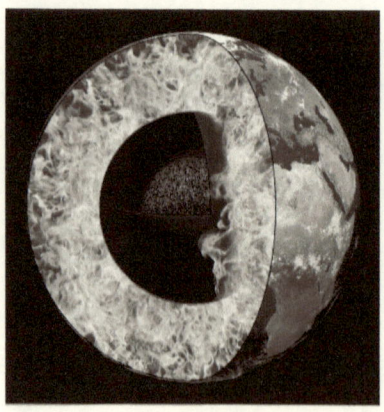

The Beach

I love to walk on the beach at dawn
with the sea air parting my hair.
As I say hello to the morning sun
I let out a happy yawn.

I love to feel the sand on my feet
as it smooths out the calluses beneath.
As I move along my beach retreat
I feel so complete.

I love the water crashing the shore
and saying "excuse me" with a mighty roar.
I keep wanting more and more
of the beach I care so much for.

When it is finally time to go
I will miss all that I adore.
For the beach is my new beau
who I will always want to explore.

Fish at Play

I love to watch fish at play
dancing the day away.
Like a group of children on a playground
they giggle and jump, and swim around.

If I look real close I can see them smile
as they glide atop a water wave.
When it's time for dinner
their mother calls
and they all get in line as they wiggle away.

The Air We Breathe

The air we breathe
gives us life.
Sometimes it can be dirty
and give you strife.

When it's clean and fresh
it's the best
as I can breathe in deep
and fall off to sleep.

But when it's dirty and stale
it can make you ill
and you don't want to inhale.

Let's make it safe
for the human race
so we can remain in this place.

Soaking In the Sunshine

Soaking in the sunshine
on a deserted beach,
feeling the rays
from head to feet.

With the sand on my back
and my face turning black,
you may think it's a macabre act
or maybe that I'm a maniac.

But you can't beat the feeling
of the radiating tingling
from the glistening sun
until you become overdone.

Desert Storms

Desert storms are nature's way
of saying we need to clean up our stay
on our fragile earth
before things really go astray.

Overusing our natural resources
by poor farming, grazing,
and deforestation allows
the wind to destroy our land.

Swirling clouds of sand and dust
can get in your eyes
making them hurt
and making you choke on the dirt.

It's also the name of a US war
fought to free the Kuwait nation
from evading Iraqi forces.

Both definitions show the devastation
these things can create.

It's up to us to do what we can
to come up with a plan
to save this earth.

Spring

As winter turns into spring
it's a beautiful thing.
As cold turns to warm
we free up our arms.

As flowers begin to peek
from their deep sleep,
the bees begin to eat
from their sweet treats.

As newborn birds open their mouths
their mothers fly in to feed their beaks.

But soon it will be over.
As the earth continues to pirouette
and the rains continue to flow,
I begin to feel my summer glow.

V: THE FINAL STREAMS

The Mind

They say the mind is a terrible thing to lose
but sometimes you need to lose it to find your groove.
Not with psychedelic drugs or royal Gorilla weed,
but with self-introspection and loving creeds.

To feed it with negative thoughts and self-doubt
only serves to diminish your clout.
The way to enlightenment is to be devout
in mapping out your way to a superior route.

Just make sure you can achieve your highest payout
while ensuring you don't suffer a blackout.

Life's Setbacks

Setbacks in life are inevitable.
Nobody scores a perfect 10
or continues to roll a perfect 6.

We all have failures in life.
But there are some benefits to failure
as long as it doesn't wash us away.

It makes us humble and open
to learning and listening
for a better way.

It makes us search within
with an objective bent
on understanding our true intent.

If we take advantage of our setbacks
to make a comeback
that would be a worthwhile payback.

Soap Opera

You treat our relationship like a soap opera
with all the drama of a cow in heat
while putting my feelings on the backseat.

Like the repetitiveness of each series,
the conflict seems to go on and on.

Don't be so restless
that you need to guide us to a cliffhanger.

I may not come back for the next episode
and take my show on the road
if this situation continues to erode.

But alas, I see that you need to continue to act
so my love for you will not be back.

Don't Back the Wrong Leader

History is alive
with people who have decided
to back the wrong leader.

A leader who is determined
to forsake his country's needs
for his own greed.

This does not bode well
for the nation's survival
as it pulls the country apart
into divisive rivalries.

It is not in people's best interests
to continue to enable a tyrant
who will eventually fall
from the public's grace.

Also, history will not be kind
to those who support a disgraced ruler.
When we look back into time
it won't be just that leader
who is held in disrepute.
It will also be you.

Ode to Bob Dylan

Bob Dylan is an American treasure
whose messages challenged us to measure
the societal norms we were writing in ink.

He sang about changing social institutions,
imploring us to find the right solutions,
which were secretly blowing in the wind.

He has made many important contributions
by forcing us to open our eyes to the injustice
of our racist, bias, and exclusionary culture.

Unfortunately times have not changed enough
as significant improvements have been stalling
and progress is being rebuffed,
which shows us that a hard rain is still falling.

Soliloquy in Black

Who am I really?
Am I black or am I human?
What is the different?
Should there be one?

I feel the same
and I'm not ashamed
of my darker looks.
Why am I treated
in a different way
when black skin
started this race?

I don't understand the mindset of this land
to undermine our common DNA strand
which originated from the same grasslands
in the vast African plains.

There has to be a better way
for us to engage in this day and age.
How do we move to the next level
to keep the racism devil at bay?

There must be light at the end of the tunnel
where we can all live and play as one pack,
but I haven't been able to solve the puzzle
but I will continue to give it a crack.

It's worse than I Thought

As a black man growing up during the segregated south
I believed the country had now seen the fallacy of their thoughts.

But when I see black men not being able to breathe,
I realize its worse than I thought.

When I see that black men were imprisoned at a much higher rate than their numbers would dictate,
I realize its worse than I thought.

When I see that a black man watching birds requires a call to the police,
I realize it's worse than I thought.

When I see black men being gunned down even though there were no guns in sight,
I realize it's worse than I thought.

When I pay for a purchase at a drug store and the cashier feels the need to call the manager to check my $20 bill to make sure it is real,
I realize its worse than I thought.

When will we all be allowed to breathe?

In Harm's Way

Please don't put me in harm's way
by leading my heart astray.
I am putting my trust in you
to see from my point of view.

I don't want to commit
if it's not your intention
to reciprocate.

It's time for you to decide
if you want to take this ride
into the sunset with me.

Mind Streams

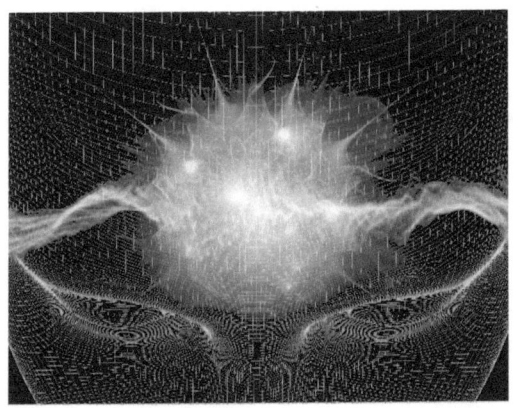

My brain synapses are firing on all cylinders
allowing my neurons to transmit my thoughts
farther downstream.

As the wave of thoughts flow freely through my veins
I begin to think on a higher plane.

 Like the theatrical performance of a summer play
I orchestrate my thoughts into a mind ballet,
choreographing my theater of the absurd
until sauntering to the final word.

Enjoying the dance, artistry, and dialogue
of my mind stream sends my consciousness into
freefall as I rejoice in the beauty of it all.

Thank You

I was 14 years old purchasing perfume for my mother when I dropped the package walking out the store. When I turned around to replace it, the sales clerk told me, "You broke it you bought it." To the store manager who ran after me to give me a new one anyway, I say THANK YOU.

I was 8 years old when I got my foot stuck in the train tracks when a train was coming and I couldn't free my foot with my younger brother watching from the curb and no one else was around. I finally decided to accept my fate and prayed that my brother and parents would get over me being run over by a train. To God who spoke out to me to untie my shoe which led to my escape, I say THANK YOU.

I was born to two wonderful parents and great siblings who have supported me throughout life. For all this I say, THANK YOU.

Easy Guideline for Giving

If by giving to others you only experience
a little bit of discomfort to achieve a major positive impact,
just do it.

If you are well off and you wonder
if you should help someone who is not as well off as you,
just do it.

If there is someone in need
and you can help,
just do it.

If you witness an injustice
and you can help correct it,
just do it.

If you can do something to leave this world
in a better place than when you got here,
just do it!

COVID-19

Can we survive this dreaded disease
Or will it destroy our future dreams?
Virtually all of us must focus our rage,
Invested in defeating this plague.
Death to the pandemic, find a vaccine!

Senior Lives Matter

There seems to be an opinion by some
that it's okay for older people to die
from Covid-19.

What happened to the old days:
When maturity was prized?
When the young cherished the old?

Is it wise
to trivialize
the loss of our elders
and the knowledge they possess?

Lest we forget,
the beauty bequeathed
to the human sect
is the sanctity of life
we have as human beings.

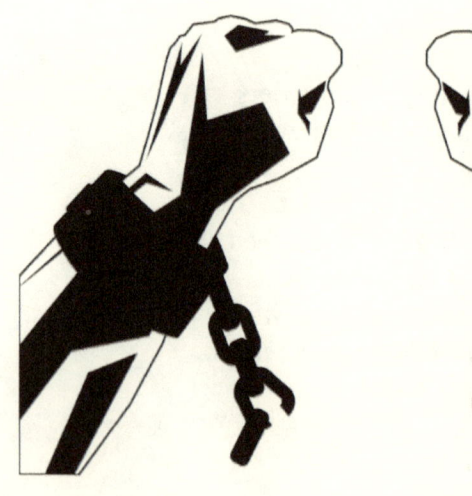

The 4th of July Is Not My Holiday

The 4th of July is not my holiday
because my black ancestors
were still enslaved.

Though this day represents
independence and freedom
for white people,
my people were still
treated like human chattel.

The 4th should be celebrated for
it's an important day for these United States
but it's time to
follow through with a
celebration for me too.

To make things complete,
and to show grace
for the past oversight,
we need a national holiday
for Juneteenth.

Small People

Small people think in tiny ways
with their bias thoughts and mental haze.
They discriminate against others
when they should treat them like brothers.

With their wicked ways and closed minds
they are a cancer on mankind.
It's up to us to limit their basal spread
by squashing their thoughts until they are dead.

We cannot cater to their religious creed
of hate and bigotry to our human breed.
We must eradicate their evil on our race
for all of us to live in God's grace.

Peace

People need to support each other,
Even if it's hard to do.
All it takes is a little will,
Combined with the strength to execute.
End the conflict and start life anew.

Dig Deep

When you are finding it difficult
to get up in the morning,
dig deep.

When you are up late finishing
that last term paper
and getting sleepy,
dig deep.

When you are close to finishing a race
and are beginning to get tired,
dig deep.

When you are recovering from an illness
and feeling too weak to move,
dig deep.

When you lose your job
and can't find the strength to find a new one,
dig deep.

When you are trying to recover
from the loss of a loved one but can't,
dig deep.

When you think you can't go any further,
dig deep.

By digging deep into your soul
you may uncover a hidden strength
you didn't know you had.
Savor the discovery.

That's Not Me

That's not me.
The one you are trying to make others see.

There are always outside forces
that for whatever reason,
are trying to bring you down.

I am not perfect,
as is the case for all the human race,
but to misrepresent who I am
leads me to ask: What's your aim?
Why do you seek to defame?
Is it to make yourself feel greater?
Do you have a demon within?

I have no problem exposing my blemishes
but I disavow any falsity from a *frenemy*.

Please don't spread your sham.
My only wish
is to present who I really am.

The Dark Side

We all have a dark side.
A shadow side with primitive desires.
A side of lust, jealousy, and tangled wires.
A side no man can deny
but one he hopes no one can spy on.

It's the other side we try to incrust.
The light side.
The side of love, admiration, and trust.
The side we hope is robust.

Don't open the door to your dark side
and if you are already inside,
come out and close the door.

For if the dark side takes over
the bright side will be pushed over.
Don't be a victim to this disorder
because you may not be able to recover.

Just remember to stay the course
and favor your bright true self.

Behind the Looking Glass

Behind the looking glass
is the soul I seek.
I see a reflection of me
but is what I see the real me
or who I want to be?

Others may see me in a different way
but they may keep their thoughts to themselves.
For they may not want to tell me what they really think
for fear of me calling them a nasty heel.

To find myself I must be willing to see
through the looking glass to a great degree.
For if I am able to achive this scary feat
I will see the person I really am.

The Harlem Hellfighters

The Harlem Hellfighters brought terror to the Germans during
WWI with their fierce fighting and French guns.
They fought back the Germans with tenacity and aplomb
even though the Germans were firing bombs.

They marched into France with their razzmatazz
while astonishing the French with the sound of jazz.
Coming from Harlem, Brooklyn, and Queens;
they were African American men ages mid-40s to teens.

They moved against the German shells
making the Germans think they were fighters from hell.
As they fought with the French to regain world peace
they attacked the enemy like a game of chess.

They fought longer than any other American team
which made their accomplishments stand supreme.
For their efforts they were awarded French metals
but in American they were treated more like rebels.

They faced racism and segregation upon returning home
like they had some kind of syndrome.
But one of them was recognized after he was a goner
when President Obama gave him the Medal of Honor.

These were the men who helped save the day
so the world could be a better place.
The world's fear was made much lighter
because of the bravery of the Harlem Hellfighters.

The Fate of My Dreams

I remember the dreams I had.
Like little tadpoles filling a pond,
my dreams were my future bond.

But as I grew older I began to see
that realizing my dreams was not to be.
Like wild salmon swimming upstream,
my dreams were swallowed up by bigger things.

Pick Me up Lord

When I am feeling down
and can't get up,
pick me up Lord.

When the road is long
and I am out of gas,
pick me up Lord.

When my voice is suppressed
and I can't speak,
pick me up Lord.

When I am hungry
and can't eat,
pick me up Lord.

When tears are in my eyes
and I can't see,
pick me up Lord.

When all seems lost and hopeless
I will put my faith in you Lord
and Stand by you.

Why Do You Disparage My Race?

Why do you disparage my race?

Is it based on hate?

What is going on
in that crazy space
between your ears?

Is it based on fear?

If you can't stand the heat
of the competition
admit it and stop your beef.

Good grief!

You will not break me.
I will not take this lying down.
I will fight for my right
to be an equal partner
in the human race.
I will not give in
until I win
this fight.

If I am cornered
I will not roll over and
I won't back down.

Rise Up

Rise up people
to the injustices of this world.
We all play a role in
bringing things under control.
We need to make it our goal
to make sure everyone
shares equally in the load.

Rise up black adults
to protect your children's future.
Rise up black children
to let the world know
you're paying attention.

Rise up white adults
to show that you are fair.
Rise up white children
to show the world that you care.

It's time for everybody to rise up
and take the fight
to the old world order.
One side cannot do it alone.
We must do it together.

The first thing we need to do
is admit that there is a problem.
For if we continue to claim
that there is no systemic issue,
we will continue to flounder.

If you don't get on board
you will be left in the dust
as momentum is flowing
and you will be crushed.

This is not about one race,
it's about the human race.
Because if we all are not free,
no one is free.

So get on the freedom train
and we can all ride together
for the common cause.

Downstream

When I look downstream
as far as my eyes can see
my thoughts flow back to me
telling me what my life could be.

I feel as if I have been washed away
without being able to stage my life's play.

In these latter stages of my existence
I would like to have a larger say
in shaping this world I live in today.
For no one knows what my future holds
during the afterlife of my D-Day.

The only thing I can do today
is place hope in my religious faith.
For if my beliefs are really true
I will realize life anew.

The Final Frontier

We have overstayed our welcome on planet earth.
As the natural resources are beginning to be displaced
it's time to move the human race to a different place.

As the fish and seafood leave the seas
what's next is the birds and the bees.
When the lack of drinking water dries up the earth
our plants and animals will bite the dust.
Once our oxygen levels begin to recede
we will know it's time to leave.

I hope we find a new earth at a quicker pace
to move our population to a more habitable place.
For we may not be able to support the people we have
for too many more years.
So it's time for us to crank up our gears
and look for another sphere.

**If your life is going downhill
make Godspeed
to the uphill section.**

- Henry Lee Thomas

VI: FLASH FICTION STORIES

The House

I felt that I was being watched as I moved around the house. I was in the center of a big circular room with eight doors equally spaced around the perimeter.

Door 8 had an exit sign above it and a window, but I could not see out of it.

The other doors were numbered 1 through 7. Being the sequential thinker that I am, I proceeded to enter Door 1. Room 1 was very dark with a dim light in one corner. A baby boy on all fours was in the lit corner looking up at me. To my surprise the baby became to speak.

"Why have you entered my room?" he asked.

Ignoring his question, I responded with another question, "Who are you and how can you talk at such a young age?"

He proceeded to tell me. "I was left here. By who, I don't know, but I was given speech so I could talk to you when you came in."

I wondered how he knew I would enter, but instead just asked, "What are you supposed to tell me?"

"Beware of the dark side," he said and then he crawled into a corner and seemed to disappear.

Confused, I left that room and entered Room 2. This room had a dark side and a light side. There was something in the dark side but I couldn't make it out.

In the light side, there was another door. I could hear a boy behind the door singing "The time is a-changing." I tried to open the door, but it was locked.

The person inside then said "Who goes there?"

I replied, "My name is Future. Who are you"?

He said, "My name is not important, but I know you. You are on a mission and you just need to be true in order to make it through."

With that, the sounds begin to wade while hearing the boy walk away.

I made my exit and entered Room 3. Room 3 was mildly lit but there wasn't anything in it! As I focused on the walls though, I noticed that they seemed to be pulsating in a slow rhythmic motion. As I got closer to the walls, their pulse rate increased and began to pulsate in a manner which initially looked random but on further inspection, they appeared to be communicating with me in Morse code. The walls were talking to me!

I was able to make out the message: "Look for the scroll". I thought to myself: *What is the scroll?*

I was as confused as ever when I entered Room 4. Room 4 was dark and cold with a red light in each of the four corners. In each corner, there was also an item: a skull, a moving rocking chair with another skull on it, a dead cactus, and a broken clock. But there was no scroll.

This room made me uneasy and felt evil as I thought to myself: *What is the meaning of these things?* I did not want to take a chance of disturbing these things because I was starting to feel like I was in a trance. So, I advanced out of that room in a hurried pace.

Room 5 was covered in hives with a large bee looking down at me. The bee began to say to me, "Beware, beware!"

I asked, "What is it that I have to fear?"

The bee looked down at me and said, "Be careful where you go and stay on the path."

This was beginning to get to me and I wanted to flee, so I decided to get going.

Room 6 was dark except for a blue light above a small round table. On top of the table was a brown scroll which appeared to be made out of papyrus.

There was a pathway which led to the table with the scroll. I could not see past the edges of the path as everything outside of the table with the scroll and the path itself was pitch black. I remembered what the bee told me and stayed on the path as I approached the scroll.

There was a long ribbon tied around the scroll with the following words written on the ribbon: Do not open. Carry to the Wise Man.

I picked up the scroll and started to pull the ribbon to open the scroll, but then I stopped and wondered: *Am I being true to my mission? Is opening this scroll taking me to the Dark Side?*

I stopped pulling and removed my hand from the ends of the ribbon then proceeded to leave the room, being careful to stay on the path.

As I entered Room 7, I noticed there was a slight mist in the air. There was an old man on the left side of the room and another one on the right side. Both men were sitting on a stool. *Which one of them is the Wise Man?*

I scanned each of the men and noticed that the one on the left had a dark shadow behind him while the one on the right had a light behind him. I decided to go to the one who was backlit. He looked 500 years old but he had no wrinkles. Light seemed to radiate out of his head.

I asked him, "Are you the Wise Man?"

He answered, "I am wise in the sense that I seek the truth and I reflect it back pure and unaltered".

He then told me, "You have made it this far because you did not touch the skull, rocking chair, dead cactus, or broken clock in Room 4. Doing so would have taken you to the dark side."

Relieved, I handed him the scroll and asked, "Will you read this?"

He opened the scroll and read, "You have been looking for answers near and far. The answers lie within."

The scroll then went up in a puff of smoke and both men disappeared. The whole room was now lit in a bright green light.

As I exited the room I was back in the big center room I started in, still wondering what it was I had learned.

I exited the house through Door 8 and walked outside into the light. As I cleared the grounds and looked back, I could see my face looking back at me.

At this point I realized that the house I had departed was my mind and that the answers were always there: *within me*.

Gone At 73

My grandmother ascended into heaven at age 73. Big Momma was a big woman and lived with us and she used Snuff.

Snuff is a powdered form of tobacco which many black women use to 'snuff' in their mouth and suck on. It had a sort of sweet-musty smell to it, but it looked nasty. They would spit it into an old tin can or cup when they were finished sucking on it and if a container was not available, they would spit it out on the ground if they were outside.

She seemed to watch the soap operas all day, including *General Hospital, Days of Our Lives*, all of them. They called them 'Stories'.

She never exercised except to walk from her bedroom to the living room, to the kitchen, and the front porch. I generally love to exercise.

When a character on the 'Stories' was hiding behind a door spying on another character, my grandmother would yell at the television: "Can't you see him behind the door?"

I always thought to myself: *That's crazy! They can't hear her!*

She passed away on that porch she loved to sit on. I loved my grandmother, but I didn't realize it until she was gone.

Gone at 73, which is an interesting number. If you add the two digits together, you get 10. She was a perfect 10 as grandmothers go.

I have been thinking more about her lately as I get closer to the age she passed. Especially since I have not been exercising lately. I don't use Snuff though.

I wonder if I will perish at the same age as her. I am currently 63.

Ten years to go…

The Lucky Charm of My Success

I never had any luck shooting free throws or bowling until I found my lucky charm.

I had the type of body build and general athletic ability that should have made me more successful with these activities and I practiced all the time.

I was out hiking one day and saw a shiny object sticking out of the dirt. I picked it up and blew the dirt off. It looked like a coin and was made out of some type of metal but it was shaped like the Lucky Charms breakfast cereal.

I found it in the dirt and my name is Dirk, so I declared, "This must be my lucky charm!"

I put the charm in my left pocket since I was left handed and rushed to see if my basketball and bowling abilities had changed.

Immediately, I was making free throws like a pro. I rushed to the bowling alley next and was hitting strike after strike.

I was so confident that I entered a free throw and bowling contest that were being held the next day.

The next morning, I put on the pants which held my lucky charm and the other clothes I wore the previous day. I didn't wash them because I didn't want to change anything that would change my luck.

I was awesome! I placed first in shooting free throws and second in bowling.

When I emptied my pockets after getting home, I realized I didn't have my lucky charm! My wife had emptied my pockets and washed my clothes and forgot to put my lucky charm back in my pocket.

Maybe I didn't need my lucky charm after all.

Who is My Father?

I was the problem child in my family. I had one sister and one brother, but they didn't look like me. They were white as ice with blond hair and blue eyes just like our mother, whereas I looked more Italian. I had olive skin, dark hair, and brown eyes.

It was us and our mother. We never knew our father. Mom won't tell us anything about him. She would only say, "He's not here and he's not a part your lives, so you don't need to know anything about him. Live in the present!"

I was the black sheep in my family. I guess I rebelled more because I was different. I didn't like being different. It made me dislike all things different.

I didn't like people with bigger houses than ours, with different languages, or with different foods. I didn't like different people. I especially didn't like black people because they were the opposite of my mother and siblings.

I decided that I would secretly look for my father by performing a DNA test. Since I was male I convinced my sister to take one as well so we would have both a male and a female test and to double our chance of finding a match.

We submitted the tests and waited for the results, hoping that we would get a match with our father or at least one of his relatives.

The results can in! We both received a report that stated "This person is expected to be your father." We were excited but when we compared reports, we saw that the name of our father was different.

I contacted the person that my report said was my father with 99.2% probability. He responded and agreed to meet with me. He only lived 5 miles away...

As I arrived at the agreed to place at a bench in a local park, I saw a man sitting at the bench with his back to me.

When he heard me approaching, he stood up and turned around toward me.

My eyes met with this tall black man with features like mine.

Dad?

ABOUT THE AUTHOR

Henry Lee Thomas is a *"Renaissance man"* whose skills and interests span many areas. He was born in Georgia but has lived in many regions of the United States and has traveled throughout the world.

He is a poet, engineer, musician, photographer, and observer of life. This diverse background, along with his introspective way of thinking allows him to see poetry from a unique perspective.

He has a B.A. in Mathematics from Oberlin College and an M.S. in Operations Research from the University of Iowa. Henry's other books are below:

Men's Guide to Being a Single Parent: Different Animal than Women Single Parents
ISBN-13: 978-0615990668
ISBN-10: 0615990665

Poems in the Keys of Life
ISBN-13: 978-1-970144-00-0 (Paperback)
ISBN-13: 978-1-970144-01-7 (Hardcover)

What Did You Think of Mental Streams?

First of all, thank you for purchasing this book *Mental Streams*. I know you could have picked any number of books to read, but you picked this book and for that, I am extremely grateful.

I hope that it added value to your life and was a worthwhile read. If so, it would be really nice if you could share this book with your friends and family by posting to Facebook and/or Twitter.

Also, if you enjoyed this book and found some benefit in reading it, I'd like to hear from you and hope that you could take some time to post a review on Amazon, Barnes & Noble, or any other place of purchase. Your feedback and support will help this author to greatly improve his writing craft and make his future books even better.

Thank you!

The Beginning of The Future